Sunshine and Shadow

Sunshine and Shadow

The Amish and Their Quilts

By Phyllis Haders

The
Main Street
Press

Credits and Acknowledgments

The author wishes to acknowledge the special help of Becky and Lee Baxter, Jonathan and Gail Holstein, Paige Rense, Stephen Elliott, my mother, Mrs. Marietta Wittkamper, and the many Amish women who have shared their knowledge with me.

I wish also to express special thanks to my aunt, Mrs. Helen Glen.

All color and black and white photographs of quilts are by Richard Champion except for those appearing on pages 19, 23, 31, 34, and 71. These are by Helga Photo Studio. The quilt details have been photographed by Richard Champion with the exception of two details taken by Stephen Elliott on pages 30 and 70. Stephen Elliott is also responsible for the black and white photographs of the Amish which appear through the book, save three illustrations. Two, pages 17 and 19, are by Mel Horst Photography, and a third, page 3, is from the Library of Congress.

All Rights Reserved

Copyright © 1976 by Phyllis Haders

Library of Congress Catalog Card Number 76-5094
ISBN 0-87663-236-3

Published by Universe Books
381 Park Avenue South
New York City 10016

Produced by The Main Street Press
42 Main Street
Clinton, New Jersey 08809

Printed in the United States of America

Cover design by Lawrence Grow

To Richard and our children, Stephen and Jill

The Amish and Their Quilts

Amish quilts are now recognized as being unique. Those made prior to 1940 were conceived through the utmost simplification of design elements, simplified to the point of abstraction. Materials were chosen from fabrics and colors acceptable within a community which religiously shunned the outside world. From this narrow disciplined background emerged a distinct and rare color sense. Within the time span of only a few generations this unique form of expression flourished and has since disappeared, perhaps never to return. Such quilts are now sought with the same determination displayed by pioneer collectors of American folk art during the 1920s and '30s and are being acquired by collectors and museums throughout the world. The territory of the Amish—Pennsylvania, Ohio, Indiana, Illinois, Missouri, Iowa, and beyond—is scoured for the earlier traditional designs. Fortunately, it was not always so. Both for the Amish and "outsiders" in what is termed the "English" community, there was a golden age before discovery, a time when quilts were worked in natural materials, dyed with vegetal or European colors, and displayed with a lack of self-consciousness befitting their naïve execution. These were the days of my childhood.

Indiana in the 1930s was still rural in landscape ·and feeling. Elwood was a farm town where quilting was enjoyed as a useful pastime for women and young girls. It was here that I became familiar with the quiet ritual of quilting—going to my grandmother's scrap bag of leftover fabric, choosing solid and printed pieces that could be worked into interesting squares, sitting back absorbed and happy as Aunt Helen, my teacher, calmly explained how they could be pieced together. Quilts were on all the beds and tucked away for especially cold nights or special occasions.

They were of an endless variety of patterns and designs, and although each had a distinct character of its own, these became familiar objects to me.

In 1935 we moved to Cincinnati, and I left behind the simple rhythm of country life. Yet, a love of quilts, their many colors and forms, stayed with me. And it was only natural that my mother continued to make beautiful quilts for my two sisters and me. Each summer I went to visit Aunt Helen, then living in Howe, Indiana, near the Michigan border. These were the happiest of days, and it was then that I was to discover the strange world of the Amish, of brilliant color and deepest gloomy black, of sunshine and shadow.

My first impression was one of shock and a tinge of fear of the unknown, the eerie feeling of looking into another world. Although I had lived in areas not unlike theirs, their world was not mine. Who were they? Why did they wear such odd clothing and dress alike? Why did they speak a foreign language? These were questions with which Aunt Helen had to cope. Even the name *Amish* was strange sounding. The overwhelming black monotony of their clothing did not make a pleasing impression on a fun-loving girl. But I loved the sturdy grey and black buggies drawn by graceful and spirited horses and appreciated their beautifully-kept farms. And one day I saw hanging from a clothesline next to an Amish

homestead a quilt of breathtaking beauty in color combinations and shades never encountered before—violet, red, turquoise, and blue on a background of black. The pattern was stark, simple strips of color gracefully flowing over a somber background. I would have to get to know these people who were capable of creating such strange beauty.

I have never ceased in my search for understanding. Hundreds of quilts from the past have passed through my hands, many as exciting in composition and coloring as the first Amish quilt seen in Indiana. I have watched the art of quiltmaking decline as synthetic fabrics and modern dyes take the place of wool from family sheep and colors from plants and German manufacturing sources. But this lamentable fall only intensifies my desire to know more about the masterpieces which I and others collect and about the people who created them. Each fine quilt has a story, and in its telling much can be learned of the Amish.

The special qualities of Amish life are sustained only through separation from the world in which we live. An intense sense of community is bred from shared customs in dress, work, and worship. To approach the Amish, particularly those belonging to the most strict Old Order, then, is to invade their privacy, to ask them to break, at least momentarily, from the proscribed ritual of their disciplined life. Because these are a gentle people, it is sometimes possible, however, to indulge one's own desire to know

and experience something of their past and present existence. Aunt Helen has known them well as a schoolteacher, and through other friends and family I have been fortunate in meeting a great many I am happy to call friends. No exact knowledge, however, can be obtained from these most unassuming of people. As with members of any peasant community, values are implicitly understood and accepted. The patterns of their lives which emerge in their work—whether it be in quilting or farming or worship—are not debated or analyzed. As members of a primitivist Christian community, they interpret all of life's activities through the narrow prism of Scripture.

Out of the darkness, out of the self-imposed blackout—the discipline of greys and blacks—shine a few unmistakable signs of an unconscious symbolic life. Almost all forms of the decorative impulse are denied to Old Order Amish fundamentalists. The interiors of homes are plainly furnished without curtains, ornate furniture, or other worldly appointments. Electricity and other modern power sources are, of course, absent from the dwelling. Except for a few pieces of decorated china and flowers in the windows, the only source of color in the home may be found in quilts used as day bed and regular bed coverings. A treasure trove of similar textiles are most likely to be put away for use on special occasions such as weddings, neighborly visits on alternate Sundays, and worship services held in the home bi-monthly. Again and again on such quilts are repeated the geometrics of diamond, square, and triangle. Out-

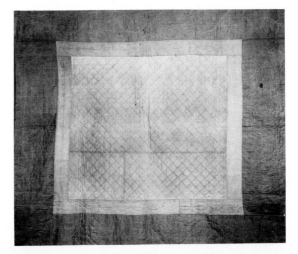

Square, wool, 76″ x 82″, c. 1860, Pennsylvania. A pure Amish quilt design with pale green center, maroon inner border, and brown outer border.

side of the house these same shapes may be found cut in the walls of barns for ventilation purposes, but no hex signs of the Pennsylvania-German variety are present. The only external colorful accents are those completely natural to the fields, flowers beds, and woods.

It has only been in return trips to Indiana and in visits with Amish friends in Lancaster and Berks counties, Pennsylvania, that I have seen so much of the unique creative expression of these people emerge and take on meaning. As the strangeness surrounding these kind people has disappeared, a respect for their way of life, their ideals, and undemonstrative love for each other has immeasurably increased. Knowledge of the Amish is, like their quilts, pieced together of fragments large and small. It was in the vicinity of Howe and La Grange, Indiana, that the Hochstetler quilt, handed down from generation to generation, first came to my attention. Illustrated in color on page 27 and in black and white here, it says much about Amish history and craftsmanship in America.

The maker of this quilt, Susan Hochstetler (also spelled Hochsteller), was a direct descendant of one of the first Amish immigrants to America, Jacob Hochstetler. Coming from Switzerland in 1736, he settled first in Lancaster County, Pennsylvania, and in the 1750s moved to Berks County. Several thousand Amish today are descended from Jacob. Susan was a member of the fifth generation, born in Somerset County, Pennsylvania, in 1826, and married to Joni Miller in 1844 in Holmes County, Ohio. They moved on to La Grange County, Indiana, in 1851. It is believed that the quilt was almost totally finished in Ohio, only the corner stars being completed some years later, in the 1850s, in Indiana.

Some parts of the Hochstetler family story are shared by other immigrant American groups during the eighteenth and nineteenth centuries, especially the movement West away from civilization. This migration was necessary for the survival of the Amish as a distinct cultural group, but religious division among the Amish themselves also caused such dispersal. In 1693 the Swiss bishop Jacob Ammann had broken the Mennonite movement into two when he refused to follow a milder form of "shunning" or avoiding those who would not follow strict Anabaptist practice. Many of his

followers, henceforth known as the Amish in Switzerland, Alsace, and the Palatinate, moved to the New World in succeeding years. Here more divisions would occur, the major one being between Old Order and "Church" Amish. These distinctions have been maintained to the present day, the Old Order adherents holding to the practice of worshipping in the home and not in a formal church structure, the prohibition of missionary work, and the practice of foot washing. As America became more and more industrialized, further divisions within the Amish community appeared over such matters as the use of gas-driven engines, electricity, and ways of dress. Yet, the Old Order settlements continued to grow and to prosper in their isolation. Today, the baptized members of the sect, all adults, number over 50,000 in more than twenty states.

Why did the Hochstetlers move from Pennsylvania to Ohio and on to Indiana? Susan was one of ten children, and land had to be found for all sons, if not sons-in-law. There was no alternative such as moving to the city and seeking a job in an English-speaking business. Then, too, there were religious divisions in Pennsylvania and Ohio, often involving the shunning of fallen faithful, but the exact nature of these disputes is uncertain. When Susan and Joni Miller moved to Indiana, they were accompanied by her father and mother and other members of the family. If only in numbers, they could easily found a new community. When Susan's father, Joseph, died in 1893 in Elkhart County, Indiana, he left his 10 children, 120 grandchildren, 213 great-grandchildren, and 19 great-great-grandchildren.

Susan Hochstetler's eight-pointed star quilt has been treasured by three generations of the family since her death in 1897. In design and execution, it is quite unlike that found in domestic American quilts of the same period, particularly those employing the Lone Star motif. Only two colors —glowing red for the star and deep blue-black in the background—suffice to suggest a blazing light. The formation of the star is unique as each of the eight segments appear as whole pieces of fabric cut in large triangles and then join to form the star. This is an intricately-worked quilt, but overall the impression is one of great simplicity. The design, as in other Old Order work, is purely nonrepresentational or geometric.

What was the inspiration for the design? This is difficult to pinpoint. The Amish themselves are unable to name sources. While designs were borrowed from other American quiltmakers, it is reasonably certain that they drew many of their basic ideas from sources at least as old as the sect itself. The eight-pointed star and the diamond are almost always found enclosed by a square, a fence (or *Zaun* in German), which carefully contains and frames such brilliantly colored shapes within an ordered system. The star is itself a symbol of prosperity and fertility; it is also the Biblical "star out of Jacob," the star in the East. It is a symbol as primitive as Amish society itself. "No other foreign nationality in America," Joseph Downs wrote in the 1940s, "remained so homogeneous or so faithful to its old-world customs and manners as the Palatines (as they were called on the ship lists)." Tapestry-woven and embroidered textiles which used very similar nonrepresentational forms were "recreated . . . by means of simpler techniques without loss of the inherent sentiment, love of nature, and spiritual symbolism of the original forms." Almost every scrap of the Amish tradition in Europe has been destroyed or has disappeared. Susan Hochstetler's star, it can be argued nevertheless, is no more a product of the American frontier than are the many anonymous diamond, square, and bar designs of other Old Order quilts. An implicit understanding and grasp of historically-based and approved forms, of traditional motifs, is at work here among a people who have lived strictly by a rule book written nearly four hundred years ago. "Folk art," it has been written, "is primitive because it is not objective; it is a return to older, more primitive and exotic forms in which the inner expressive forces of reality are as yet undistorted by the conscious mind." Such naïve art is that of the Amish quiltmakers.

The gathering of information on Amish quilt types is exceedingly difficult due to the reluctance of persons to speak about them. A vast body of lit-

Sawtooth Diamond, wool, 80″ x 82″, c. 1920, Pennsylvania. A popular variation of the diamond design often found in Pennsylvania.

erature exists on the textiles of the primary Pennsylvania-German immigrant groups; writing on or by the Amish regarding decorative arts and crafts is almost nonexistent. Adding further confusion and complexity to any discussion of crafts are the differences in method and nomenclature between the Amish of different states if not communities within a short distance from each other.

Amish quilts, especially those made in Old Order settlements prior to 1940, can be considered singular, nevertheless, in several respects. The most important of these is the use of especially vivid colors and combinations of them. In addition, designs, whatever their derivation, were always worked in a nonrepresentational manner. Only in the quilting stitches do likenesses of flowers and other earthly forms take shape. The designs, as has been stated, are not always original with the Amish. Use of a central medallion device such as the diamond is repeated in English and other American quilts of the eighteenth century. Did the Amish copy these? This is possible, but it is more likely that the form was one with which they were already familiar. And in actual practice, the designs became quite different. Amish women did not appliqué them; rather, they let color and fine stitchery define the outlines and play of shapes. This they continued to do well into the twentieth century. In non-Amish circles, the central diamond quilt was considered hopelessly old-fashioned by the mid-nineteenth century.

That quilting has played an important role in the lives of Amish women for at least two hundred years, however, is a fact that cannot be disputed. This activity has afforded women creative and social outlets denied in other areas of domestic life. Why was it allowed? Probably because the quilt has been viewed as a utilitarian object. The making of quilts is a natural extension of other matronly duties performed by a wife and daughters such as the making of clothing. Nothing, of course, is wasted in an Amish home. Until recently most clothing was made at home, and the scraps from these projects were saved for use in aprons, towels, pin cushions, and quilts. Sometimes special pieces of material were received as gifts, and these often ended up in finely worked quilts. Such an example is illustrated on page 59. These may have been patches of silk brocade, delicate ribbon, or velvet. The primary materials used, however, were cotton and that most domestic staple, wool.

Wool is a fiber most receptive to color; it invites brilliant and subtle effects. It was the perfect medium for the Amish quiltmaker. Although

these people present a very sober, monochromatic face to the world in their outward dress, bright colors are not foreign to them. The brightest may be worn in the form of dresses under their dark garments. Others are found in men's and boy's shirts. "Although the Amish are more conservative than the Mennonites, who allow printed and dotted materials," one writer has observed, "the Amish colors are far more brilliant than those worn by Mennonite women, who choose light grey, coffee, and dark shades, along with 'quiet' prints and polka dots. Amish dresses are often a vivid shade of blue, green, wine red, or purple, although older women frequently cling to black, dark grey, and tan. The material is always a plain color, never checked, striped, or printed, and even polka dots are considered too 'gay' and worldly."

Why are such bright colors chosen for use in quilts? Without indulging in pop psychology, it seems reasonable to suggest that quiltmaking itself is an escape from the monotony of rural life, the humdrum tasks of raising a large family. Life has been very hard for the Amish, however large their private income. Because they deny themselves the implements of modern life, it cannot be otherwise. But it need not be and is not deathly dull. Quilting bees are themselves important social occasions in these peasant communities; for generations neighbors have silently vied with each other to create the most beautiful and original of bed coverings. Why not then make use of strong, stirring colors? Why not quilt a royal purple patch

Sunshine and Shadow, wool, 73″ x 75″, c. 1910, Pennsylvania. A more common arrangement of squares than that found in the quilt on p. 51.

18

next to one of shocking pink? As long as the end result is not worldly in appearance, too fancy for a plain farmer's wife, no sins of vanity and pride are committed. Contained as they are by the vocabulary of strict geometric forms, there is little likelihood that servants of the Lord will go astray while working with the needle.

Bricks, trundle quilt, wool, 52" x 52", c. 1890, Pennsylvania. An elementary pattern worked in vivid reds, blues, browns, and cream.

It is the juxtaposition of colors which strikes the eye most forcibly. When I saw my first quilt in Indiana, I wondered to myself, what kind of woman would dare such a combination of colors? These are not the cheap pastels of modern times, but slashes of cardinal red and mauve, emerald green against turquoise, violet played against blue-black. It is probable that only a people isolated from general society for many years, members of a true ethnic sect, are capable of such original expression. To some extent the quilts constitute a bold statement of independence from the tedium of earthly existence, but they also affirm the value of a disciplined way of life.

Boldness in the use of color is usually matched by restraint in quilting designs. While often displaying considerable technical skill, the stitches are modest and used mainly in outlining basic pieced shapes and in creating simple patterns. The latter are designs which in large part seem to

have originated with the Quakers of Pennsylvania. Chief among them is the "Quaker feather," a design of plume scrolls and wreaths. Other favorite Amish quilting patterns also recur in Quaker and Pennsylvania-German work in general—roses, tulips, single stars, and stars within stars, clusters of grapes, leaves and tendrils, primroses, baskets. Hearts were used by the early Amish quiltmakers for bridal quilts, and were not as frequently encountered as today. More complex elements such as lilies, bows, pineapples, birds, and shell quilting are less often found. Some Ohio and Indiana quilts are dated and/or initialed; those from Pennsylvania with such stitched details are few in number.

The quilting was performed in a manner common to all such fabric coverings. The top of the Amish pieced quilts were sewn together to form the desired overall pattern. Lines for the quilting patterns were then lightly drawn on the top in flour, chalk, or soft pencil. Templates of cardboard, tin, and even wood were often used to trace the patterns. The twisted rope or cable design is one pattern that was often so mechanically outlined, often by one woman especially skillful in placing the quilting patterns. Other patterns were drawn freehand. This top and two additional layers, a filling or "batting" of cotton or wool and a bottom or "backing" of plain or printed fabric, were put in a frame and stretched taut, ready to be quilted.

The relatively open forms and large spaces of the traditional quilt design allow for a considerable display of stitchwork. Some of this is totally independent of the overall top pattern, but most reinforces and enhances it. This is particularly true of Susan Hochstetler's work in which the quilting resembles the most delicate type of embossing. The quilted circles radiate from the star and accentuate its shining quality. On the other hand, Mahala Yoder chose to decorate her oblong quilt with birds, stylized stars, and classical urns or lyres. Each element appears to have been rendered freehand.

Borders on Amish quilts are usually an integral part of the overall design. These are not applied until the quilt has been removed from the

Mahala Yoder, *Oblong,* cotton, 63" x 86", 1909, Indiana. Black background with violet borders and back—the essence of Amish simplicity.

frame. Borders are formed by one of three methods: bringing over surplus fabric from either the back or top and stitching it down, turning both edges in and stitching them together, or by adding another strip of fabric around both top and back. This is the method most often used by the Amish. It is evident that much thought is given to a proper choice of border size and color. It is this frame which finally fixes the quilt in its composite form.

Once completed a quilt is used in ways in keeping with its utilitarian function—as a cover for beds, cradles, trundle beds, and sometimes day beds which served as couches. Every Old Order Amish family opens its home for church services at least once a year, and a particularly fine display of quilts may be displayed at this time. Not all quilts, of course, are used immediately. Some are intended for a daughter's dowry or as bridal gifts, and these are stored away. Also used only for special occasions such as services, weddings, and funerals are those family heirlooms which have gained the respectability of age. It is important, however, to emphasize that quilts are not put on view as art objects. Indeed, one of the few quilts I have found displaying an appliqué pattern (a simple leaf traced from nature) was being used as a padding between the springs and mattress of a bed.

Certainly there is a fondness if not a love for quilts which animates both makers and users of them. But once the simple pieces of wool and cotton have become familiar objects, it is likely that they will be laid aside if not forgotten. Even some of the most treasured of these antique coverings have been sold to outsiders. The Amish family auctions, special social occasions for the whole community, are the place where quilts are often presented for sale. Here they may be bought by other Amish and then resold.

Outsiders are rarely allowed to attend family auctions, but friends may intercede. My husband and I have come upon such affairs and have been invited to observe them. They are happy, festive occasions, affording a wonderful opportunity for visiting and feasting. There are sandwiches, shoo-fly pie, and homemade sassafras tea available. The bidding and buying of objects is spirited. It may seem ironical that these least materialistic of people should take such a delight in acquiring new possessions. The auction, however, serves a salutary function in "recycling" what are basically used objects. They also serve to settle estates when both parents are deceased. "The children shall meet together," a document reprinted in the Hochstetler family history reads, "[and] all articles [named] shall be divided amongst the said nine children in peace and love or sold to the highest bidder and the greatest articles which will run high into money, my executors shall give to him that is lowest in inheritance." The executor of the estate is most likely to act as the auctioneer.

Several times after both public and family auctions, an invitation would be extended to return to the home of a participant. In Shipshewana, Indiana, I would find myself involved in a long discussion of such a pattern as that known generally as the "basket." Did I know that the symbols were really hands with six fingers, and that Swiss ancestors had been born with such limbs? The pattern was called "hands" and not "baskets." Was I aware that the design called "Drunkard's Path" was known to the Amish as "Solomon's Puzzle"? These small and curious bits of folk knowledge were shared with regard to my "outside" interest. Particularly in conver-

Hands, cotton, 68″ x 80″, c. 1935, Indiana. Deep navy blue background with red inner border and one red "hand" in center row, third from left.

Baskets, cotton, 78″ x 80″, c. 1910, Indiana. Multi-colored typical designs on a blue-gray background with red border.

sation with older Amish women, I would discover depths of untutored wisdom and an intuitive understanding of folkways and customs.

Yet in Ohio, Pennsylvania, and Indiana I would almost always meet with the same inability to understand my interest in "old" quilts as compared with those on which they were actually working. The women could not understand why I did not think the new white background, polyester-filled quilts made from kits and patterns were unique. Several offered to "copy" the old ones if I liked them so much. My explanation that such an imitation would not be "original" was never really understood.

A bishop in the Old Order sect, a man holding the highest pastoral office in an Amish district, once attempted to explain his people's philosophy with the simple explanation: "Ich bin ein Bauer. Wir sind Bauern." *I am a peasant. We are peasants.* Little thought is given to why a custom is followed; few will elaborate on the reasons for subtle changes in methodology. It is sufficient that form be followed, that the rule be obeyed. "To question the rightness of these customs," one authority on the Amish has written, "is equivalent to denying the very nature of religion." Quilting is such a customary activity, but royal purple has given way to baby blue, cardinal red to pastel pink. Rayon and polyester are replacing wool and cotton. The quilting itself may be expertly worked, but not as finely.

Many quilts are now being made to sell. The outward form remains, but the inner spirit is changing, and few will ask why.

As I look back on my own childhood, part of which was spent in Amish country, it is clear that even our "outside" world was simpler then. How much simpler, accordingly, was the living style of the Amish? Their separation from commercial society was not totally complete, but they did exist in relative isolation. For over two hundred years the Amish woman relied on her lively imagination and gifts from nature to brighten her somber home with comfortable textiles. There were no synthetic fabrics or quick-set commercial dyes with which to fashion clothing, and hence, from scraps, quilts. It is not to be expected, then, that the unique contribution of the Amish should continue indefinitely as if the world around them had not changed in the slightest respect. The miracle is that this peasant society survived so long free of self-conscious creative expression. Like the hymns of their beloved *Ausband* which have only recently been transcribed into measured stances, the quilts of the past will remain graceful, inspired, and evocative reminders of an important cultural legacy. And for those of us who cannot directly share the Amish experience, they stand as singular works of art.

Star

There shall come a star out of Jacob, and a sceptre shall rise out of Israel.

Numbers 24 : 17

Susan Hochstetler, *Star,* wool, 74″ x 86″, c. 1848-50, Holmes County, Ohio. As striking and simple as the Amish center diamond quilt, the Star is equally symbolic and representative of this Germanic peasant culture. The star blazes forth from the darkness with an intensity unmatched in American needlework. Unlike the Lone Star pieced quilts of the nineteenth century, it has been designed and worked as a totally unified symbol in one color. Although some of the eight segments forming the star were pieced as many as six times, they seem to have been fitted together only once. Such was the maker's skill that the thousands of small stitches are absorbed into the texture of the quilt, giving to it only a subtle shading of color and texture. So finely has the feather-circle and diamond-and-square quilting been worked that the quilt appears to have been embossed rather than stitched. The growing progression of the feather-stitch circles contributes to the illusion of the star expanding beyond its limits. But as with many other central symbols in Amish quilts, it is clearly contained by a simple square. Here the color is deeper yet, suggesting the deep blue-black night that lies beyond the four eight-pointed stars of the border.

It is perhaps not surprising that this evocative creation should have been the work of a member of one of America's leading Amish families, the Hochstetlers. Begun in Holmes County, Ohio, it was carried by Susan Hochstetler Miller to La Grange, Indiana, in 1851, and handed down from one generation to another. Made primarily of a woolen fabric known as Henrietta cloth, it was carefully preserved as the treasure from the past which it is.

27

Diamond

You are fellow saints and members of the household of God, built upon the foundation of the apostles and prophets, Christ Jesus being the chief cornerstone, in whole the whole structure is joined together and grows into a holy temple in the Lord.

Ephesians 2 : 19-21

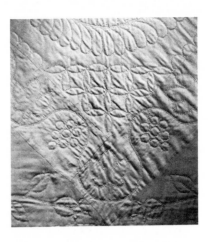

Diamond, wool, 78″ x 78″, c. 1900, Lancaster County, Pennsylvania. The diamond—in old German usage the *eckstein,* or cornerstone— stands as a singular aesthetic symbol of Amish culture. Frequently repeated in pieced quilts and often colored a brilliant scarlet or red not unlike that found in medieval costumes or pre-Gutenberg woodblock-printed playing cards, the diamond possesses unusual symbolic strength. It was not a design element born on the American frontier. The diamond is here used with exceptional boldness. Juxtaposed with turquoise, deep blue, and moss green, it demands strict attention. Perhaps only with the use of wool fabrics, in this case challis and twill, can such an intense play of color be realized. The black-thread quilting is similarly strong. The center diamond consists of a feather circle filled with squares. Framing the diamond is a second such form worked with grapes and leaves. Each of the four triangular blue corners contains a single rose in full bloom with leaves and a rosebud on each side. Grape and leaf quilting is repeated in the square turquoise border. The verdant green background is filled with finely stitched feather scrolls. Each of the quilt's elements is as carefully arranged and worked as the next. Taken as a whole they constitute one of the masterpieces of Amish culture.

31

Ocean Waves

O that thou hadst hearkened to my commandments!
Then.had thy peace been as a river,
And thy righteousness as the waves of the sea.

Isaiah 48 : 18

Katie Gingerich, *Ocean Waves,* wool, 62″ x 80″, 1901, Ligonier, Indiana. The Amish were not reluctant to adopt non-representational quilt designs from other cultures. This design, however, is rarely seen in Amish work. Borrowed from New England sources, it assumes a new form with the use of very subtle colors—rose, violet, mauve, purple, beige. All are greyed in shade, melting into each other in perfect harmony. That such a cohesive statement was achieved is no small feat. The quilting is surely the work of several women in addition to Katie Gingerich who signed and dated it. The outline quilting defining the waves, the flower design in the solid brown squares, and the undulating feather scrolls and tulips in the borders are executed in stitches of different lengths. They are not as uniform or as small and precise as those found in a quilt completed by one woman. Taken altogether, however, they strongly reinforce the designer's intent—a feeling of outwardly contained but inwardly flowing movement.

Bars

Strait is the gate, and narrow is the way which leadeth
unto life, and few there be that find it.

Matthew 7 : 14

Bars, cotton, 81″ x 87″, c. 1910, Tuscarawas County, Ohio. As straight as the furrows plowed by the Amish farmers of the Midwest, this quilt design is also known among the plain people as "stripes." As simple a form as is to be found in nature, it defies representational analysis. Color builds upon color to form precise squares; only the luxuriant green bars threaten to break up the perfect proportion of shapes, but these are restrained by the purple bands which relate to the larger world of the same color. The quilt displays a thoroughly disciplined approach to design, but one in which the surprise and excitement of life are not excluded. The bars of both colors are quilted in simple diamond shapes. The red and purple borders contain a graceful primrose and leaf pattern. The quilt is backed with a printed cotton in shades of blue.

39

Diamond

This is the light of the heights,
This is my Jesus Christ,
The rock, on whom I stand.
Who is the diamond.

Amish hymn

Diamond, wool, 80″ x 80″, c. 1900, Lancaster County, Pennsylvania. One secondary and two primary colors are used with extraordinary effect in this most simple of Amish designs. It is truly overpowering in graphic impact. The center red diamond stands as a cornerstone, a symbol which ties all others together. It is first set in a field of emerald green which harmonizes with the blue diamond border but also sets the red center apart as a singular element. The red square border reunites these elements, as does the larger blue square and the red binding. Fine, detailed quilting appears throughout. Typically, the red center is stitched with a feather circle or wreath, within which are stars. A small rose with leaves is outlined in each of the diamond's corners. The blue diamond, as well as the first red border, are quilted with primroses and leaves. Found concentrated in the lush green corners are full-flowering roses, rosebuds, and shell quilting. Graceful feather scrolls are stitched in the blue outer border.

43

Double Nine-Patch

Awake, O north wind; come, thou south;
Blow upon my garden, that the spices thereof may flow
out.

Let my beloved come into his garden, and eat his
pleasant fruits.

The Song of Solomon 4 : 16

Double Nine Patch, wool, 82″ x 83″, c. 1930, Lancaster County, Pennsylvania. Amish flower gardens are every bit as colorful and orderly as this field of diamonds. Working of pieced quilts and raising of flowers are two of the few creative outlets allowed Old Order Amish women. The design is not unique with the Amish. Use of nine equal squares or diamonds to form a block, five of these also broken down into nine equal squares or diamonds (Double Nine), is found amidst other nineteenth-century work of varying American origin. What is unusual is the handling of color. Purples, greens, and pinks are of an intensity not encountered elsewhere. These work in combination with blues and reds to subtly define shapes. The plain blue diamonds hold everything in place. Those in vibrant green surrounding the center field suggest a fence that protects the garden from disorder. Quilting is limited to four-petal flowers in the small solid diamonds, to the green diamonds of the border, and is interspersed with the flowing feather stitches of the outer purple border. An unknown quilting pattern appears in blue diamonds.

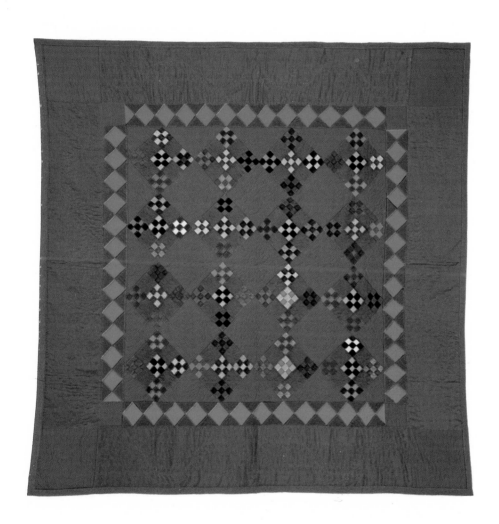

47

Sunshine and Shadow

We pray, O Holy Father, that we might leave behind the night of sin and guilt and ever walk in the shining light of Thy wondrous grace, and cast off the works of darkness, put on the armor of light, and walk honestly as in the day.

Amish, *A Devoted Christian's Prayer Book*

Sunshine and Shadow, wool, 80″ x 80″, c. 1920, Lancaster County, Pennsylvania. Out of the darkness and into the light, the traditional Sunshine and Shadow design reflects the rhythm of rural Amish existence, the eternal renewal of life itself. An exceptionally orderly, tidy way of life, its calendar is continually informed by spiritual considerations, a striving to live by the behavioral guidelines of the *Ordnung.* Planting and harvesting, the baptism and marriage of a son or daughter, the joyous birth of a baby, the solemn death of a revered elder—all are events or activities celebrated by this pietistic, peasant culture. If the natural order is broken by the departure of a member of the flock, the community is plunged into a period of darkness, of mourning. The family of the wayward child laments its loss as a death not to be followed by the victory of the Resurrection.

So it was for the mother who made this quilt for her only daughter's dowry. She refused baptism and at age twenty-one departed for a "worldly" life in the nearby "English" town. The quilt and others handed down from generation to generation were sold. "Our girl Sarah chose not to follow our ways," the mother sadly explained. The quilt, however, remains a statement of better days, its bold pattern of multi-colored diamonds building gradually upon one another against a somber background. The daughter has been "shunned," but the miraculous survival of Amish society is affirmed daily in households across North America.

51

Log Cabin: Cradle Quilt

Be fruitful, and multiply, and replenish the earth, and subdue it.

Genesis 1 : 28

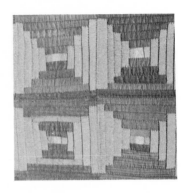

Log Cabin, cradle quilt, wool, 36″ x 43″, c. 1860, Lancaster County, Pennsylvania. A cradle quilt is easily identifiable because of its size; the dimensions are often half those of a regular bed covering. The quilt is, of course, lighter in weight. In the hands of the Amish, these differences are accentuated, particularly as they appear in the Log Cabin motif. It is not a design original with the Amish, but it is evident that they have made it their own. The "log cabin" is a house in its very simplest, almost non-representational form, each of the pink squares serving as a chimney, each strip representing a log. Bordering the cabins are slightly-angled bars which suggest the plowed fields. The many shades of black, brown, and green—from olive to deep blue—of light and dark, blend to create the log cabin form. These are punctuated in true Amish manner by the addition of vivid pink accents. The same shocking shade appears in the outer binding. As with many other quilts of the Log Cabin type, the top and back are joined with simple stitches outlining the rectangular strips. There is no filler or interlining between the two sides.

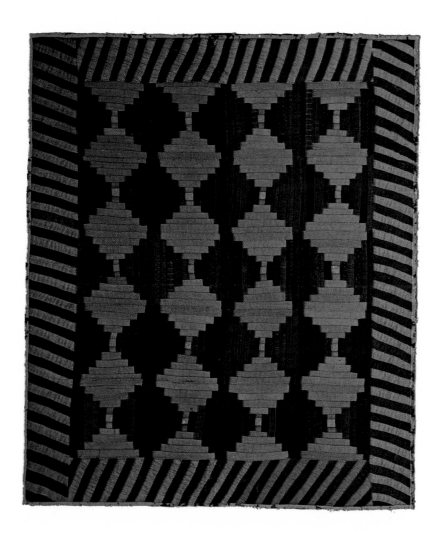

Fans: Friendship Quilt

Finally, be friendly to all and a burden to no one. Live holy before God; before yourself, moderately; before your neighbors, honestly. Let your life be modest and reserved, your manner courteous, your admonitions friendly, your forgiveness willing, your promises true, your speech wise, and share gladly the bounties you receive.

Amish, *Rules of a Godly Life*

Lizzie's, friendship quilt, primarily wool and cotton, 66" x 76", 1899, Topeka, Indiana. On May 10, 1899 sixteen-year-old Lizzie Amanda Sundheimer was invited to a quilting bee in an Amish home. An orphan since the age of eight, she lived with various relatives who provided her with the guidance and love that mark any Old Order homestead. Because Lizzie was considered a "sweet and sunny girl," her friends in the community turned to quilt-making to pledge their devotion. "Forget Me Not," "Remember Me," "Think of Me" were some of the simple sentiments embroidered in the individual squares. The names remain, too, along with Lizzie's—Katie, Ida, Sarah, among others. It is said that there were once other good wishes, other names, but that these were ripped out when a church deacon proclaimed that the design was a "little worldly." It is. The embroidery or decorative stitches are unusual enough on Amish quilts; the color fan shapes are positively exuberant in shade and texture. While primarily of wool, the fan strips also make use of fine cotton and even a few heavy silk brocades and ribbons. Cherished and rare bits of cloth were brought to the task of pledging devotion. The quilting, as in many other Amish pieces, is a subdued and graceful feather pattern. A single tulip appears at the base of each fan. All that strikes the unpracticed eye, however, are the strong bands of color employed in a patterned manner. When Lizzie Sundheimer first saw her friendship album in cloth only the quilting had yet to be completed, and this was accomplished in one day. It was, one witness declared, the "best bee ever sat."

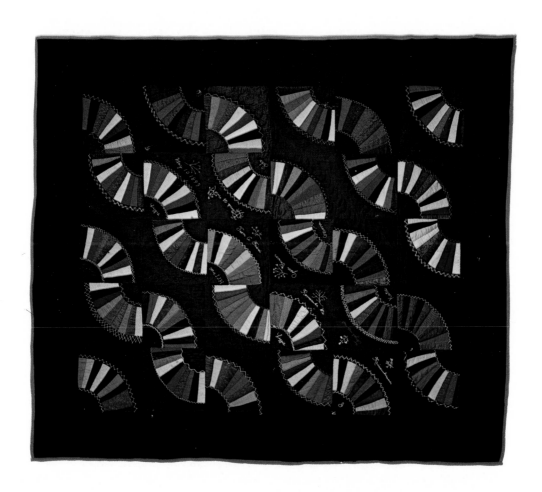

59

Honeycomb

And I am come to deliver them out of the hand of the
Egyptians . . . unto a land flowing with milk and honey.

Exodus 3 : 8

Mattie Yoder, *Honeycomb,* wool, cotton, and silk, 70″ x 78″, c. 1910, Honeyville, Indiana. Elements such as the diamond, square, and rectangle dominate the Amish design lexicon; these are among the most ancient of motifs. Broadening and enriching the scope are an assortment of symbols drawn from a life led close to nature. Although without realistic outlines or distinct and graven imagery, these are forms which are identifiably inspired by the physical world—long, straight bars of solid color stretching out to the limits of the horizon like the lines of a plowed field, the hexagonal cross-play of the honeycomb. Appropriately, this quilt was fashioned in the midst of the fertile northern Indiana territory of the Amish, in a community known as Honeyville. It is an exciting, exuberant composition, making use of some rich and printed fabrics. These worldly pieces, according to local tradition, were given to the quilt's maker, not purchased or worn, and therefore could be used without fear of disapproval. The primary materials pieced together are, however, of lightweight wools. This is the medium of the pinks, reds, blues, yellows, greys, blacks, and turquoise. Although the diffusion of colors looks to have been arbitrarily arrived at, there is an order, a sense to this swarming honeycomb in the juxtaposition of one color with another. Each of the hexagons has been diamond quilted. Surrounding the square is a moss-green field with wide cable quilting.

63

Diamond: Bridal Quilt

O Lord, almighty merciful Father, in Thy eternal wisdom Thou hast decreed that it is not good for man, created in Thy image, to be alone. Therefore, Thou gavest him a helpmeet, a wife taken from his side, that the human race might be increased and uncleanness prevented.

Amish, *A Devoted Christian's Prayer Book*

Diamond, bridal quilt, wool, 83″ x 83″, c. 1895, Lancaster County, Pennsylvania. As resplendent in color and unified in design as the finest of ecclesiastical vestments, this quilt was made for a simple but spiritual purpose in the Amish family—a bride's dowry. The hearts quilted throughout the piece designate it as being intended as such a gift, perhaps from mother to daughter. Only the initial "K" embroidered in red thread in one corner of the backing gives any hint of the maker's identity. This anonymous artist created a quilt of unusual graphic strength and expression. The vibrant diamond center relates perfectly to the square of similar shade. The four blue diamond corners, each quilted with four hearts, reach beyond their borders to the great blue field which encloses the whole. Brown, magenta, and, finally, green dramatically emphasize the play of red and blue, of diamond and square. Worked through the wool in simple quilting are such motifs as seven- and eight-pointed stars, a feather circle, clusters of grapes and leaves, a rose and buds, shell baskets containing a single tulip, and hearts. The wool backing, often unrelated to the quilt pattern and colors, is in the case a square of deep navy blue marked with tiny white dots, a work to be admired in itself.

67

Cross Within A Cross

And whosoever doth not bear his cross,
and come after me,
cannot be my disciple.

Luke 27 : 14

Polly D. Yoder, *Cross Within a Cross,* cotton, 70″ x 80″, dated March, 1914, Shipshewana, Indiana. More complex and mysterious than many designs used by the Amish, the Yoder quilt follows a well-defined design tradition. Yet color and form are exceptionally well-articulated and coordinated. If you draw a horizontal or vertical line across the middle of the quilt you will see how the elements are systematically repeated. What religious meaning should be ascribed to the design? Probably no more or less than that accorded to seemingly "secular" forms. Everything treated by the Amish has more than mundane meaning, but little is made explicit. Diamonds and triangles form both a Gothic-style and a square St. Andrew's cross. Almost as important a design element are, however, the plain light- and dark-blue diamonds and triangles. Focus only on these and you will see a totally different design. Simply outlined flowers are quilted in the plain dark diamonds and the outer border. The extension of the dark-blue diamond color in the piece to the right defies any aesthetic explanation. Polly Yoder may have simply run low on grey-blue cotton for the border.

71